Starting a Conversation:
Poems and Prose

By William D. Sloofe

Printed in the United States of America
Akmaeon Publishing, LLC
309 Firkle Ferry Road, Ste. 209
Cumming, Georgia 30040

Copyediting: Martha Chaney
Cover Design: David Stanley
Cover Art: Christina Johnson
ISBN: 978-0-6928611-2-7

Table of Contents

prologue

i will wait for a while
to see her smile
the smile in my memory
i may not know what love is
i know what it is not

लोवे

Love is a force. We cannot command love. We cannot demand, or take away love. Just as we cannot command a sunrise or sunset. Love is calm and forgiving. Love demands a place in time. Love is bigger than us. Love strikes like lightening - unpredictable and irrefutable. Like the sun, love radiates independently of our fears and desires. Love relaxes our spirit and love redeems our soul. Love is inherently free. It cannot be bought or sold. Love has no borders. Love has no mass, but love can fill a room. Love can change the world. Love knows these words before I write them. Love is inherently compassionate and empathic. Love is absolute and infinite. Love honors the sovereignty of each soul. Love has brought you here to me and me to you without reason and continues the same.

sequence

if for nothing
give me a smile
i love your smile
you are the smile
in my memory
my hazy dreams
become reality; in thought
thought in reality and are different
when subject to careful stability
of looking at myself
today
the hands of time change
words explain
words confuse my mind
my words are so escaping
it becomes fearful
today is no longer
those dreams are the same
what was then?
is the possibility
not forever
for its passed
tomorrow is on the horizon
still, in the mind are memories caught
not forgotten,
relived, remembered and realized
for love is a bond of no end
i hold you close to my heart forever

leveling

time pushes away the evening
leveling the earth to another day
my thoughts are gathered
the page is set
words expect nothing
less than perfection
in their solution to answers
left unspoken
i toil through my thoughts
music reminds me
i am not alone here
though i have never been
closing my eyes
i take a breath
piece together
what is left in my memory

new day

you think of me
when my words reach
past time
but tomorrow of my
tomorrow
words will not rely on today
but will exist with the ages
before i go
remember
i love your smile
& wish tomorrow was different
i don't know where we go from here
so, when i go
remember me with a song
words that stumble
into the delicate majesty
of a new day

paths

my feted path of dirt and stone
unknown until the morning of my defeat
love doesn't exist in the moment i live
but exists in my dreams
spirits counted of days gone by
history to never repeat
a summer's day
a cabin retreat
alone with everyone i meet
my spirit cries a thousand times
waiting to retreat
to your arms
in passionate grasp until
the morning repeat
whispers torn from my lover's scorn
of nights without me
challenges still of the future appeal
journeys accompanying me
arguments still of truth revealed
of the causes that destroyed me
silent still of truth revealed
of your love for me
a memory
i know the treat of a heartbeat
when you lie beside me
come closer please and remember me
whispers retreat
if i am really where your heart declares
a final defeat

vital

breath to hold
your eyes cut across the room
to my attention
the rhythm of my pace increases
my thoughts are fluid
i try to pick them up
like leaves in the autumn wind
little success
redemption and self-control
lost on the day
the mind stumbles in the darkness
the path is enlightened with passion
of not knowing
hope shows the way
it's a moment
unexplained in silence

sheets

back again to redefend words from yesterday
missing a friend i did not intend to lose
time does not retreat and history does not repeat,
saying i love you falls silent
but as our lips close the distance
your eyes tell me how to move
deep into another moment
either i am too young or too old to remember
how your touch freed my muse to these words
my body lies in the softness of flannel sheets
cool autumn air fills the room
it is where i want to be among the words
that describe you
hold you close to my dreams
my soul is no longer separate in the fog
i know these thoughts won't go away
these words fall to deaf ears
you have no room to appear
in the story of a different year
the heavy morning clouds
hang close to where i can reach
of the breath i take in fainted dreams
soon to be departed words
woven into the fabric of passion
i await for you to return to the room
though you have just stepped away

unfolds

my heart beats a thousand times
i sway in the wind of a song
i listen more intently
draw my thoughts to the words
closely - it's one life
my soul hurts
while the path grows wider
time steals from my youth
given back in memories
growing older
only what i intended
the reality of
yesterday remains silent
as the songs play
to be beside you
tomorrow unfolds
dreams are told
in the echo of today
am i to cry as you walk away?
smile as you come closer
touch my hand?
dream as you kiss me?
a cool breeze reminds me
... it will be okay

go

no point to remember
what i didn't know
words are not carved in marble
from a long time ago
no history held with time
pieces of granite unknown
except to those who wander
the places they call home
so my name is on the wind
held upon the trees
places i have never been
doubt i will ever be
it's hard to choose words
those not used or said to me
no words for history books
no traditions
no traits
what is left for tomorrow
what i make today
integrity though of a life to go
in behind those dreams
meant to be
the absence of light
is not always the end

fate

reach out to the cruel fate of time
past the flicker of light
carried in dreams
faded by the brevity of life
the forgiveness of song
closing my eyes places me back
into a memory
the rest shared with you
only to be whole while we're together
lost within the distance
what is written to the ages
left and visited no more
alas our youth has passed
yesterday is filled with darkness
tomorrow cannot shed light
looking back to the absence of dreams of tomorrow
i choose to leave
allow your mind to recall
memories you have of me
in the end the world has worn me down

hearts

you no longer hear the words
written in rhythm and song
fighting the battle of time
stealing my words to explain
where we've been
of a life before to complain
perfect plan to understand
times unseen - misunderstood
what the future holds is absurd
i realize who we were
when love was in our hearts
too young to know
that tomorrow comes
yesterday goes
trip and fall to return to the paradise of words
and the comfort of a drink
my mind relaxes
my heart still sinks
in the shadows of looking back
and to return - impossible

solemn

alone with you in my heart
the solemn silence of yesterday
stolen unattended
i cannot rely on your smile to make me happy
but your memory cuts deep
in the passion of your silence
words hang in the air of what should be said
i know who you are;
silent as the past
celebrates your mystery
your symphony plays as you run for the roses
brushes to paint a portrait of a life:
forgotten in your memory
moments of your solitude awaken
you walk away in the dark gray morning
settled into the fog of an autumn day
you think of a moment in time;
sip your coffee
smile adjusting to the situation
waiting for the memory to return

landscape

judas cried to the thought of divulging his
destiny unfair to history
of a life lost on a tree
does God take away the life of tomorrow to replace it?
intervene to replace the bad with good?
does scripture hold all truth for tomorrow?
am i destined to love?
be loved?
liked?
disliked?
am i to live a rich life or die an agonizing death?
easier to call out the weak than be weak
i have fallen to my knees in prayer
on the rock of st. peter a church was built
and men followed; the book was changed,
interpreted to suit the cause of another
splintered across the landscape
churches built and another
war fought
people have died too many times
in the name of God
and on what side does God fall?
those who pray first?
pray longest?
most committed?
the truth is beyond these lives.
in the end

melody

hoping you see yourself in my words written
in the silent wind as they fall desperate to defend
dreams unloved to the end of a lover's touch
back again no history to amend
if i fail to lend my thoughts to the world
lost in the end
that's meant to mend broken hearts
in a world that's going to end
should i amend my earthly goal to attend
let it be me in the end
to draw your thoughts to where the light bends
to a moment in time and not pretend
what has been love that truly matters
to comprehend a spiritual journey
i must resend a song in melody
dancing with the spirits
while my thoughts from within
call to mend a smile of a friend
before i begin
the footsteps end
in a love forgotten

closing

poetry has a way of closing itself off
my muse sets aside words that belong to the heart
passion or fate
i draw my future on your touch
i tremble when you are near
i give it all away knowing your eyes
will allow me to smile
your soul is here beside me
i feel your spirit alone with me
while i stand in a crowd
listening to music
i wonder if i can have a drink
gaze at you from
across the table; take your hand
you are beautiful, intelligent
ready for this world
though there is darkness before the dawn
i know it's going to be all right
nervous but not alone
knowing i can't even spell
when you're around
i smile thinking of a different day
your touch means that much
… and i sip my coffee and
smile, exiting my memory

before

afternoon breaks
autumn air settles to the damp ground,
you prepare for the latter half of the day
stoking a fire to warm your house
you allow yourself a moment of vulnerability
smiling in your memory of a soft touch
lacking a kiss as evening presses the day
i awoke to see the day
i am challenged by the setting sun
i put on a vinyl LP
wait for the cracks and pops of the words
as they reveal poetry in song
it's not the same dream i have had before
i wonder where you are?
landscapes challenge
we prepare for bed
you gather your thoughts
collect what you have done during the day
realizing your thoughts remain the same
night falls quickly
your body is tired but it's hard to sleep.
i too gather my thoughts
time steals another day
i am challenged
geography and circumstance
smile knowing in your absence
i will miss you more
i want to write more about this day,
but the moon pushes a new night
the sun pushes another day
i wait to see you again

retreat

words are protected by the imposture of time
the imposition of my spirit in the grand scheme
it's karma not fate
what is generally lost to the day
is gained by a night of dreams and
there is no illusion to where i stand
knowing who i am
makes all the difference
as my prose repeats
what i have lived; whom i have loved
words fall softly; letter by letter
do not retreat in favor
but capture time
moment by moment
waiting to hear your voice
kiss your lips and draw you close to me
to make another memory
belonging to this life and not in the shadows
but a reflection of what should be, what could be
i'm yours in the distance and in the past
you are the voice that is my muse
you have been there for ages
waiting to appear in my today
how long were you hidden away?
discovered and lost
seeing the world is different
while you're beside me
the shadows fall long, tired and deep
words come before and one day i will sleep
knowing my soul will rest - with you
words are protected
written, read and hidden
knowing they tell a story
about a girl i kissed

valid & unaware

wondering if i were to die
where you would be in my rhyme
stories left untold for the ages
left unwritten for the pages
only told by the whispers of angels
unaware where my soul shall live
after i shed my mortal skin
i will always find my way to you
shedding these tears for you
waiting to hold you again
i cannot go until we're done
my life will not be over
until your heart is won;
and when i seek the
fault of stars
the moon will ask
who you are
seeking to know the name
i've exclaimed
in my dying hour of my dying day
while st. peter monitors heaven's gate
seeking my soul; he too shall wait
as my spirit is beside you
and when the song is over
when the dance is done
i will find myself in ashes on the wind to roam
don't cry for me there
i have lived a good life - in love

folds

my identity is muffled
sketched into the shadows
which retract without the sun
i feel like i am falling through the air
grabbing at clouds
wondering where you are;
how can i reach out to you?
and my heart beats a thousand times
when i think of your name
when you come close to me
i watch your every move
your eyes
your hands
your hair
your smile
i know your soul as it folds into me
and in this day
as it stands there is way too much to say
for a few whispers

again

your spirit crosses the divinity of heaven
i feel your thoughts
through a friend
what was the beginning
feels like the end
alone and tired
i struggle in the moment
i lost you
knowing; i could not help
& while i have prayed
for the repeal of your soul to heaven
the truth is revealed
you're dancing at the gates of heaven
waiting for them to open: returning again
to see me when: i arrive at the station
my saved soul
i enroll in paradise with people to see
meet and greet of time forgotten
i made the journey tired
still of my last appeal
for my words rhyming
and while desperate to attend
the very end
you died alone
i cry deeply
hurting more than weeping
cannot return and never will
i won't ascend
so surely i cannot not attend
a seat at the throne of st. peter

and to attain a chair with one who cares
Jesus at his table
is only a blessing away
and i must confess
i am frightened by the mystery of faith

seeds

trees grab the sun at the end of the day
stretch their shadow across the fallen snow
they stand as soldiers against the blowing wind
waiting to defend an army they do not know
paths taken unafraid of the journey
seeking to amend my memories
i stand with my back to the wind
looking for the end of a story yet untold
paths intertwined among the woods
not trodden black of passer i do not know
duck and cover in the place too dark to see
seeking shelter among the pines
where the grass is never green
lotus flowers among the blooms
though not in tune with nature
fall dormant in the winter
too delicate to live here
wishing this place were different
of seeds never sown
places to roam away from here
of partner never sought
because there was another
dreams that went dark
whilst the moon has changed
i am out of sight but not out of mind

unforgiven

be with those i don't mention
and time forgiven in those i do
of and for a life forgotten
veterans reprise a daily grind
seen on a corner of my commute
dollars please for me to feed
a family with no future
promises made
kept the same
a government diluted
men of wealth
who dare not deal in the death of a nation
God doesn't please those in need of salvation
but better served in terms of congressional labor
of this approach the senate
took whomever came here
while my face is young
i am overdone with
buy me pay here
lessons learned though not deserved
of a place in history
could it be a part of me
was lost along the journey
from the troubled streets
my heart beats
a thousand times before for this nation
sacrificed and lost on the way
so i must stay
traveling about the ins and outs of
constitutional mayhem

where the wealthy feed on the poor indeed
while they claim another victory
no political foe in whom we know
the battle created
religion first then the church
but God didn't stay here
wondering when time and again
how i made it here
votes taken in a box
not locked ready for the taking
as a nation bleeds i am not at ease
with the direction
founders please hear the trees of the chainsaw
awakening
intervene with your spirits keen
to save our nation

a couple

these trees that are before me
are of spirits past;
lovers holding hands
that stand the test of time
wisdom, not fame; looking for serenity
they lean on the ledge; as time passes by
guarding the stones; weathered by time
they lie piled in a field
of a man's work; set to the side
so the soil could be rowed, planted and picked
to feed a family
rural to the nation but home for generations
on the black ridge
the forest washed with memories,
spirits if you please
i can feel them with us now
i can stop and speak
but they don't repeat
how they came to be here
history retreats
if we only knew
how they grew
into such a place
whispers of those
we don't know and those we do
gone before us
seeking the souls of what's intended
of spring and summer
through fall and winter
they stand alone

but together
what tales they do not reveal
in their silence
lovers still on the hill
forever

place

somehow we live in fear of tomorrow
when yesterday was tomorrow
we fear the unknown
lived for the same
songs that we sing in our mind
linger without time
chances we took before
no longer have bearing on ourselves
tears are forever lasting
in the memory of our past
but the future is different
according to the phases of the moon
so we continue in hope of another day
believing today
tomorrow and the dreams that we created

me

i've kissed her lips
tasted her smile
held her in my arms at night
i love her…

begin

you are searching for me
beyond your memory
can't place your arms
around me until tomorrow
i long for the sun to rise
a new day to begin
i encourage a setting sun
a battle to win
hiding in plain sight
waiting
willing to close the gap
knowing
you are on my mind

warmth

dreams and sunrises
the wind blows all the time on this ridge
i remember when there were no trees
now it's a forest
i remember when there was no passion
now there is love
tonight the moon rises
shadows fall silently in a cold autumn night,
leaves rustle against the ground
if you listen you can hear me in the distance
stars enter the night sky like fireflies in july
filling the night with hope
my heart beats faster knowing
the sun will rise
the warmth of a new day begins
keep a little time for me
we start another day as strangers
i travel through the whispers of love
where i hold you close to me as angels sing
your body sways with mine in the counted rhythm
i travel about all the things you're thinking about
i hold you tight when the time is right
step back to begin - again
i grew up a lifetime ago
another body to grow old but one life
though you're miles away
yesterday you were here with me
i close my eyes to tell the stories about you
smile when you're near of counted laughter
distant fear of you not returning

i listen to old songs with new words; lost in the same
meaning returning me to my youth
the future unfolds with memories to untold
in the next emprise knowing still
secrets last forever

tomorrow
(for Christianna)

her soul dwells in the house of tomorrow
where you cannot visit - not even in your dreams.
impressions and there are hardly any
that i cannot think of
i have thought butterflies are miracles
with that i believe in God
one step forward
today was enhanced by the day before
what is more likely to be a memory
becomes a dream
she is of you, from you and of God
her touch is a part of her being;
her cries cannot be translated
they are to you and to no one else
all her anguish and emotions are for you
no one can ever take that away
she grows in the sunshine of the world;
the one that brings her butterflies
and other small miracles
in her growing; you grow old
and tomorrow comes
and tomorrow comes
so the days become days
dreams you had all come true
in her growing; you will grow
in her hurt; you will feel pain
from her happiness;
you will feel happy
all of this and all of these things
will be memories tomorrow

away

nothing forced or focused
my heart hurt
thinking i may
have to give you up
silhouette of your soul
marked in my memory
my muse - unidentifiable
until yesterday
and i listen closely
to your words
like falling in love
moon is bright tonight
seeking advice
how to continue
in the shadows until
we're ready to step away
embrace is tight
i cannot fight
words i have to say
spirited of course
i cannot ignore
love at my door
and while i comprehend
my earthly end
i wonder
does it matter anymore?
resounding - yes
i must confess
no recess to explore
before another
my muse resends
words i need to say
and more

consequences

dreams are not just for sleeping
they intend to place ideas in the day
to live a life intended
it's ok to change course
if you're lost and need to find your way
in love and need to find your place
souls cross the threshold of time
making the spirit of love
in this moment in this time
knowing life is short
simple but to be sweet
needs our attention
what can be lost
can be found
but there is always a journey
in the end
it's about the first step
with no regard for consequences
there are always consequences

guilty (1986)

lacking experience, so i say
who can judge the guilty today?
knowing one, suggesting few
everyone else is guilty too
telling secrets, enclosed in lies
truth is gone - say goodbye
forever gone till time stands still
let everyone do as they will
the tomorrow of yesterday is here today
suggesting excuses
reasons for illusions
sadness may occur
hope will succeed
this part of life is good
for something
enclosed in the heavens
only spirit is gone
God will take over
we shall all carry on

memory

today
learn to love in silence
room cold and bright
sun brings
night fades
branches scratch
the windows
storm unexpected
but likely this time of year
reading a book
cover to cover
a beach somewhere
calm and unafraid
day goes on
water is warm
foaming with nature
captured in words
a photograph
a memory
put together here
sun sets
light is stolen
stars replace the sky
and shine

drums

a room
i disagree
where you are
lights of afar
across a mountain
roads to roam
twisted depth
lined with trees
called upon unrelieved
in course of time
nothing else
stands between dreams
memories cannot be taken away
standing alone
seeking a
symphony
unrepentant
wow it was played
songs from a different day
violin as intended
no drums
crimson rose
spring is here
winter gone

night

i have God's ear
he gives me a muse to proclaim
these words to your dreams
to be beside you
when geography holds you at a distance;
tomorrow deals with a different appeal
to bring me closer
while today isn't going away
it does go too soon
stand here beside me
put your arms around me,
look into my eyes
feel the dreams at night
hold me tight
between the time you have to leave
complimented
not held in reserve
you deserve happiness
scribbled here for you
these words for you
never to be taken
tomorrow please
i must agree
to the happiness in your heart
doubting still
that i may reveal
anything i have not already said
here i am
waiting for your return
you have my attention

pausing

i pause hoping i can contribute to the conversation
there is not always a story but often a dream
i cannot temper my emotions
these words go unedited
and wait for your reaction
the muse lays down words
describe what cannot be told
what cannot be explained
dreaming of tomorrow
i find you at the center
knowing the sweetest memories
were to make are still left
tomorrow envelopes nothing that i have not seen
in the words of song
i believe in the place it takes me
journeys intended on paths
that have not seen
footsteps; and i am ready for a walk
to places i have never been
so long as you're at my side
dreams intended for another day and that's ok

evening

beautiful when the day begins
with the thought of you
dreaming of you the night before
in my thoughts you reside
places i mean to be;
on a beach between work and play
an afternoon
doesn't come too soon
we share the same memory;
or dream what it means to be beside you.
i seek and i find that tomorrow
comes without regard to yesterday
all i remember doesn't go away
as tomorrow seeks a different day
to become what we say ...
all evening i intend
to dance again when the time is right,
while the music plays
it does not obey restrictions of time,
while my dreams appear
so crystal clear
tomorrow remains foggy;
obstacles still to reveal the journey
ready for the adventure

skip

considering the universe
all that's held in time
a soul that searches
the heavens for reasons and rhythm
no stone goes unturned
no fire without a spark;
it can be a lonely world
waiting for love to return
on a day so far away
words cannot always say
what my mind must obey
when you step away
to a different day;
and love left to not obey
the obstacles of time
there is a sadness in my heart;
waiting for your return
knowing your presence
won't last long,
my spirit fades into the distance
skip and stutter
wondering what tomorrow brings

sleepy

waiting to return
to my dreams
aware
holding the line
seeking truth
waiting past my youth
appearing no more
existing no less
traveled feet
nothing to repeat
living still
in the shadows
cold and dark
death retreats
love
repeats in favor
no answer here
to reappear
where tomorrow should exist
living as if today is today
disappear
when tomorrow arrives
dreams saved
for a different day

seeking grace

upon a winter's day
nothing but love in our way
singing a song
it's okay to cry
but not while i'm away
who will hold you today
listen and make the pain
go away
holding you close
to stay
perilous envy
when you go away
of the mirror that reflects
your beautiful face
upon your return
held in place
love that descends
an eternal space
of time and geography
there is no disgrace
in wanting to stay
with love
delivering a smile
wishing you peace
as your soul seeks
mine in place
for the grace of God

answer

watching the sunrise
your beauty outshines
morning glow
and the sunset
evening show
stars cannot outshine
or climb higher
than love that's divine
where to start and finish
left to believe
to succeed to be with you
converge upon my dreams
no words
kissing you softly
left to touch you
pulling you tightly
when songs
explain where i can remain
and see you in the room
recovering gently
time passes quickly
today i have you
what of yesterday
came and went
in my defense
i am not looking back
seeking and caught
my words remain here
calling you to the door
for another kiss

begins

inside my heart
a journey began
dreams demand
a fairytale end
committed until
another begins
though
fate is running late
it's not out of date
to examine what may be
a love to last forever

unexplained

as stars align
there comes a time
to fall in love
pictured here
photographs in my mind
it's about a touch
like never before
about a hurt
unexplainable
breathtaking beauty
stops me where i stand
a smile from a thought
of just
holding hands

different

if my days unfold an unfortunate way
we can't solve many problems
remembering i intend to make you smile
music plays from different days
but the message resonates
i can smell your perfume
before you walk into the room
dreaming of tomorrow
working backwards
among my scattered thoughts
to make my way on this path
silent words you have not heard
ones i cannot explain
ready for the day
night gets in the way
stars are not as bright these days
the moon doesn't compare
a sunset leaves desired words
that just aren't there
the sun rises
a new day
words don't get in the way
because nothing can be said in comparison
to your beauty

traveling

enduring still my last appeal
my last breath exclaiming your name
no complaining
i am not remaining in a place
my dreams cannot obey;
where the music doesn't play
seeking the soul of another day
to reform my thoughts upon a way
when it's April in Paris
lovers remain throughout the day
in majestic company
holding hands at a table on the street
watching and speaking
with people we meet
coffee and baguettes to eat
laughing and smiling
as the day retreats
evening repeats
red wine in glasses without reaction
i kiss you softly
offer you my coat
because it's chilly
there's a candle lit
on the table
stars hidden by the city lights
we gather our things
hand in hand
strolling the streets
talking about the architecture
i buy you a scarf

spring air is damp
flowers peak
on the boulevard; on the street
where we've never been
but we should go tomorrow

spoken

never spoken
comfort in knowing
where you are
dreams seldom told
except to you
in these words
knowing they could
be forgotten
in your memory
only written
intended for a book
of pages marked
knowing our conversations
in these words
in these dreams
as time marches on
hearing the beat
if the music that plays
for you and me
knowing we should dance
wings beneath our feet
holding hands
slowly settling
days into days
not alone
comfort in knowing
you were here
beside me
saying i love you
and not
waving goodbye

person

not sure i am ready to stop
believing in tomorrow
as time gives up
on dreams
the ivory keys softly
play a melody
a song i sing is not in key
while everything seems wrong
love outweighs
what's against me
i am lonely but in love
tomorrow comes
not a word
except in my memory
close to where i stand
imagining you beside me
trying to manage a
conversation from words of a journal;
written before
i was you and you were me
mistakenly different company
you hold my hand
scared of shadows
and reflections in mirrors
i say let it be
tomorrow
i am a brokenhearted person
the world has upstaged me
hoping time hasn't robbed me
from being in love

and i have no fear
but envy of the wind
across your face
beautiful
longing for your embrace

company

stars in the sky
but the whole sky fell
words can't escape
a tormented hell
yesterday left
tomorrow found
no wings
for the angel
no bells to ring
half the stars
don't shine
on my way home
it's half the ride i need
empty in my passenger seat
no room to suffer fools
including a life for me
but each of us has a part
still, this is no game
wondering why you step away
can't explain
and the breeze blows cold
in the morning
as i return without warning
to begin again
of words meant for time
and photographs
dreams suffer the silence of days
i am quiet when i say your name
in the company of no one
alone

what?

sometimes i want to talk
but instead i cry
you walk away
grasping my thoughts; in despair
calypso where are you?
dark days of winter
keep me here
melancholy as dreams disappear
not enough time for fate
as tomorrow takes place
will you be beside me?
on the days it rains
rainbows encounter
a sun's endeavors
in the shadows of words
never written
on paths not taken
of words unspoken
meant to say
but left for another day
closed off to time
that doesn't arrive
without this encounter
in this café; a world away
with bourbon on ice

no matter

time doesn't get involved
in yesterday
failing never considered
but what of the cost
a moment taken
day is lost
night doesn't compete
dreams fall silent
day encroaches upon day
leaving me frustrated
expectations
writing these words
seeking your thoughts
all that really matters
may not
begin again
feeling the wind
upon my face as i walk
on a rainy day
paths not made

middle

here i am on the cusp of life
looking at the edge
moving forward
looking to my side
as you look back at me
these words in my heart
find themselves in order
bringing what i have dreamt
to the day
across the night
through the heavens
arriving here
there is a journey
to each part of life,
rules to be followed
each moment accounted
until one falls in love
young or old
before or again
life can reset
another story
to begin
timeline
of this life
in these words
to tell
what has yet
to be told
there is a path
for you and me
with our future
history to make
all in a conversation

destined

i am young in my heart
not clouded with life
though i have lived
music
embraces my soul
not for control
but for love
absent
and i feel lonely
i can't feel gravity
pushing down on me
but i know it's there
not fragile
but strong
your heart
your mind
your smile
destined to be great
in love
who can wait?
life to live
dreams forgive
what time has passed
between dusk and dawn
ready to begin again
released from these thoughts
my soul seeks salvation
beyond the shadow of man
walking to a place
i already understand

i was old
but young again
knowing
i can begin
on this path

keen

others have tried
to catch my eye
and align my heart
with theirs
their words fall fair
don't compare
a love
that really matters
words for you
when you ask to view
part of the conversation
existing still
today's appeal
having you here
beside me
sights unseen
of lovers keen
but they don't matter
in your embrace
i can't escape
i don't want to
as a story ends
fairy tales begin
and fill that space
in your heart
lovers leap
with joy
to compete
space and time
endeavors

you don't know

confusion and doubt
more than i should predict
less than i can imagine
days without intention
though you intend on the day
songs without purpose
my soul hurts without this
words on lines that fall to blind eyes
deaf when ears choose not to hear
nothing left
you walk away from me
leaving me unloved
alone
left with these words
left with these dreams
left alone in this world
life goes by without you
though you're 19 feet away
looking back
you turned the corner without me
looking for a different life
insecurities set a pace
setting myself before you
intending to take care of you
put in a place i don't want to attend
september winds come again
autumn is at my door
as the year repeats
life retreats
in a dream of my fears
never spoken

pages

roads not taken
words unspoken
broken into pieces
unimagined
mistaken; for a life before
no going home
where one doesn't exist
no love
where you live
to forgive impossible
another road
across the tracks
paths set before me
can't look back
when looking forward
spirits hang in the air
looking for you there
in the book
with a turned page

footsteps

dare to stand where i stood
it's easy to make someone cry
choosing to make you smile
my demise is not written in the stars
it's carried in the galaxy
where no one has been
outer limits cannot be found
if not reached by the soul
the stars cannot shine
without your reflection
the moon seeks a different path
no one knows its true destiny
a minute at a time walking this path
a footstep divided into seconds
the beat of a new song paves the way
paths made on these tracks to a different life
running away to anywhere; without this pain
without these thoughts; words left unsaid
in a storm of life
i never saw coming
the universe has a plan
to balance what is unbalanced
that's why you are here

never knew

my words are written with perfect intention;
paths to dreams not everyone can see
merely penned with mention
taken from conversation
as i own these words
i see your face hoping they impact tomorrow
hoping the song i recommend
you hear the same way i do
not my sole intention
but not an invention of my imagination;
loving you is where i want to be
wanting you beside me
all along i believe i would find you in song;
keeping you may be the question
as life may get in the way,
hoping you will promise me
that you will be happy
knowing one day you will wake up with me
to enjoy a second cup of coffee

falling dreams

carrying a heavy soul
with a fragile heart
mortal body to depart
words not written
knowing where to start
to end is not the same
mistaken phrases of words
pulled apart
wondering how long
this will go along
or fall apart
in the auspices of love
counted phrases
of love's endeavors
on trails i have yet to see
footprints that set me free
on journeys made for me
stolen kisses in the dark
meadows of green
wet with dew
rain to depart
a walk we have not taken
perhaps tomorrow

exits

today exits slowly
folded into another
wandering in the journey
taking care of you along the way
lighting the darkness
holding your hand
finding answers
if you don't understand
i will be your shelter
protection in a storm
a blanket to keep you warm
letting you know it's all okay
you will never be lonely
where i stand is where i stood
i have been at your side
for 100 years; and this is
who i am
who i want to be
no plans without you
words will flow from this moment
today presses on
in the dawn
of tomorrow

parents

not imagined or dreamt
at my defense
you left me on the roadside
life passed us by and
i don't know you
don't know that i missed you
if i didn't know how
cannot dream without having lived
or die without knowing why
words fall back to questions
unanswered in the course of time
depending upon myself
with no one there could i depend on
in a life with no end
until i stepped away
no retreat from yesterday
my thoughts return
where i cannot be
or return where i am
not sad or sullen
no use
no excuse
what i have
earned
i have never returned
where you left me
looking ahead
no regrets
except in the time: lost
writing these words

rain

my dreams in the morning
in the evening
will you listen
words you have not heard
silence in a storm; calm in a field
walk beside me; holding my hand
without looking down
without looking around
looking ahead; no plans
10,000 tomorrows
rain falls - dawn rises
there are no
beautiful goodbyes
only tearful endings
new beginnings
to appear
space and time
coalescence is near
commanding our attention
not stumbling or falling
running and jumping
exclaiming
out of breath
knowing i lived well

nostalgia

yesterday seeks another
my memory is filled with words
refusing to go quietly into that good night
where today bridges the dark
the coalition of our souls
binds a new day with a new night
i know you came somewhere from my long ago
there is a place in my heart
that is finally filled; you have returned me
to a new spirit
as you rise to meet me at the road;
take my hand for the walk
shuffle your feet
to the beat of a new song
words left unsaid
hanging as my soul seeks a new dawn
challenged, unfettered to receive
the nostalgia of where my memory has been
every ending starts a new beginning
we'll be there in the end

commanded

afflicted by man about his dealings with God,
how does Jesus see the world we've become;
grace cannot be granted at every turn
so ask for mercy where mercy can be given
tattered and torn so a church breaks apart
builds another until ... and another
so is this a God problem or is it a mankind problem
casting stones when no stones should be cast
is this God's will that man should devise
what he can interpret from God to suit his own life
so mankind can walk in destruction
against their fellow man in the name of God
how can you condemn someone in the name of God
and then establish a new building in God's name
is this not hypocrisy?
or do we dismiss that as well?
did God intend the free will of man
to question God and rely on man?
or rely on God and question man?
i hear what my ears allow
but what does my mind allow
to be interrupted and how?
when did it become ok to step away from God
and align yourself with man's religion?
i am commanded by talking with the father
through my mind and his world.
i am not commanded by any man
souls can't be saved by man

parts

here, smiling in the sun
your words warm my heart
the thought of you; my soul
tomorrow falls gently on time
today remains a part of the mystery
i step into the question
one answer remains
i am ok with the journey
builds my character
and i miss you more
i seek to know tomorrow
i don't want to regret
saying forever ago
i loved ... but
don't want a broken heart
well enough to play the part
time is my answer
picking up small stones
i can move the mountain
ready to take on
the intended task
tomorrow will arrive
dreams fulfilled
bringing a new day
with no regrets

control

spirits push me
forward
my soul rises to meet me
at the road to take
pulling me closer
from mistakes i've made
standing without you
every breath i take
moon is full
aches in my heart
feels like i've nothing left
still a smile to ponder
from the thought of you
i am hiding in plain sight
love takes control
but you are the one
in my dreams
i've finally found you
a lifetime of searching
you're my best friend

perfect

i will leave no tithe
for man
i give
where i can
time and coin
dollars be
couldn't be perfect
not if i tried
no paths to follow
no places to hide
no angel's wings for me
but an angel still
love of nature
God and friends
places i have been
yet to be
thoughts and dreams
journeys begin
at the crossroads
where things end
taken or given
from our dreams
paths unknown
in a lover's touch
forgiveness of time
never too much
when words fall to deaf ears
blind men see
dreams in the future
not predicted
or lived, but happy

happiness

words fall gently on time forgotten
reappear in the patronage of time
taking a breath of their impact
lost but not forgotten
perhaps to be realized
when the time was right
when love was once again
in my thoughts; what tomorrow gains
yesterday lost
treasures brought by time;
dreams of the future
impact is forever
eternity is the road ahead
as the letters from these words; these thoughts
here in this time taking from what yesterday began
tomorrow allows,
today deals in the interchange of thoughts
being silent, moving forward
to ensure my soul is settled
among what seems like a bunch of jumbled dreams;
but it's never been more clear
i can see for years into the future;
struggles, hardship all possible
but there is happiness lots of happiness

storytelling

nothing more than i have gained in your love
is a happy day so more than that cannot be taken away
the puzzle piece that fits the space
is not foiled by time
as it belongs where it belongs
cannot be changed in the cruelness of time;
one lifetime is centered on living a storybook
existence without regard to happiness;
discovered and lost in the space between;
now finding myself in a different place
in the spectrum of time; so happiness seeks itself
when itself can be discovered
your smile is folded into my memory
like the end result of the puzzle
those pieces can only fit together one way
but life holds many facets and the end result is
unknown
there is no predestined outcome
one can change the path but not the past
so looking forward is the only option
existing here choosing the next path
that is where i am
tomorrow falls quickly
the storybook of our lives has no ending until we're
done
so every day is a beginning
the story goes on

still

muddled ploy in a quiet house
you're not here
i am somewhere else
my thoughts come back to you
without exploration,
you're here on my path
not interrupted
but joined in the silhouette
taken from these moments;
shadowed from yesterday
days before knowing
i have loved you for ages;
its history to explore

unencumbered

tomorrow draws close
i see where you are in my dreams
my reality has you beside me
in terms of tomorrow
no pictures taken
words have the ability to draw their own
continuing to capture each moment i recall
laying the foundation for love that is inspired
interwoven into my mind's eye
left to my aging memory
my body carries the weight of a few years
but i am heavy only in burden to make my way to you
music plays quietly in the background
i am lost in my own thoughts
my own words in a room full of people
i type and peck what my muse expects
leaving nothing
i believe until the next words appear
what can i expect?
i no longer have regrets
except not getting here sooner
destiny, a plan,
i have none at hand
today remains intact
makes me smile

bottles & oceans

maiden voyage of a ship yet sailed
secrets hidden beneath the deck
tomorrow seeks what can't be found
today lost in the journey;
seeing the stars at night on the open ocean
you know God is with you
bottles stuffed with words on folded paper;
yellowed with time
tempered with iron ink to express my love for you;
praying still my life will reveal
a journey ended
not rescinded on the path put before me
anchors released from their depths
what was holding us back; nothing left
learning that happiness is available anytime
but may require a change of course
seeds yet sown of an ocean overgrown
with stars from heaven
not found or lost - what it cost of a journey
that remains interrupted
heaven exists and angels resist
the petals that make them flowers
lost, castaway to nowhere in miles of oceans deep
the secrets stowed in a ship untold
of a life that's here before me
remaining still

dying heart (1987)

the dying heart bleeds with passion
the person letting go
was not as easy as it would seem
the destiny between the two
had not been the same as intended
now reality had struck
with a cruel memory of heartache
to believe in something
so unbelievable
to have lived something
so unreal
now in present time
using logic
confusing enough it seemed
but now it looked to have no hope
informally i asked
informally she declined
without a destine of solitude
i listened to her answer
without regret of being embarrassed
i asked again
with a pause in conversation
that seemed tense
she smiled …
staring at her beautiful eyes
that expression was told
before becoming truth
i took her hand
squeezed it gently to let her know i cared
she gave in
the memories flashed back

had she changed?
had i?
would we be the same?
i thought "no"
only with hope will we have a chance
but now i recognize
the feelings seem mutual
the night passes, we move on
the love scene plays in my head
i catch a fragrance; her perfume
the attraction that leads me to her
in the darkest of nights
i run to her; fighting my way every inch
through this life
and as she turned to my call
i took her in my arms and without hesitation
i kissed her
and as she returned my kiss i thought
what was running through her mind?
i asked without regret
she answered without hesitation
i love you
as the tears fell from my eyes i said
i love you, too
then …
i seemed to rub something from my eyes
sleep, sandman dust, from the night before
i had been dreaming
i jumped into and out of a dream
i had been asleep
the dying heart bleeds with passion
where to find it?
where did it go?
where will it end?

invite

intended
to begin once more
is to say i gave up
not what i intended
to be or not
of dreams made indeed
these thoughts compel
these words invite
love is never forgotten

less

by faith and fate
on my way to you
in these dreams
and expectations
this part of my life
from my yesterday
i saw your face before
i found your love before
in my journey here
knowing more
loving no less
how tomorrow unfolds
in my stories untold
until these words are read
these are the days
of my storied life
with you

before

as i slept
i thought of you
like many times before
i have loved you in my dreams
before my dreams existed
this love existed then
before i knew love
i wrote these words
before i knew words
these thoughts
before i could think
i felt the softness of your skin
before i could begin to remember
what has become
has already been
in my thoughts
in my dreams
in my today
in my tomorrow
i have walked with you
before i could run
held your hand
before i could dance
tasted your lips
before a kiss
in the september
of our lives

maybe

putting away words
from yesterday
briefcase born
die the same
haunts and spirits
companion fear
of you never reading
another word
you don't ask i shouldn't offer
reasons are yours to ponder
collecting my thoughts
from my darkest days
penning them now
remember no more
hard to tell
where i may be
when it all goes dark
no control of what's behind
only what's ahead
steps taken in depth
a new life to begin
what tomorrow allows
without these words
without this journey
looking over to see you beside me
smiling

clear

hard to think
minutes count
the way they do
a few days
i can't explain
the way they fall
expectations
get me every time
have i given you too much?
surrendering tomorrow
miss you too much
no time to borrow
seeking what i share
but dare look back
beyond compare
remaining clear
words fall fair
order and odds taken
not mistaken
developing into
another day

face

cold winter's day
thinking of how you warm my spirit
how your presence
fills my heart
smiling
in my dreams
you solicit
my attention
pulling me into you
holding my face
tasting my lips
clutching my spirit
holding my soul
loving me
loving you
tomorrow

perhaps

walking the day
through the wind
i am a man of words
looking for a place
to begin
ending still
mortal ashes
cemetery bins
boxes and places to be
not for me
standing in the land of the living
panhandling at heaven's gates
begging for permission
to enter
one day
culled and curled myself a place
in this world
against all i have been against
no matter
remembered in the dawn
forgotten at dusk

i am

a rested heart
a journey
humbled
realizing the world
bigger than i noticed
dreams are vast
uncomplicated
suggesting
i am smaller
than i knew
hard to find
one's place
thinking you
already found it
an adventure in life
not wanting to be alone
in my thoughts
in my today
in my tomorrow
still, i am what i say
today i am ...
perfectly me

sight

no apologies still
what i may reveal
in the words
i have for you

never

words are rarely unfolded
in silence
when my dreams are stopped
pushed back
a different meaning
of the world
restless hearts and minds
one life to live
secrets held
in the escape of my heart
tomorrow falls silent
a distance too far for you to see
where today arrives
dreams are held
close to my heart
for the reprisal
that can never start
no beginning be
that has not existed
except in the muse
of my heart

dreams

may not come true
if you don't believe
in tomorrow

tomorrow

time disregards my request
hastens a pace
today unfolds as quickly as it came
still, tomorrow rests at the horizon
my heart tells me ...
i want to be your left
and your right
your good morning and good night
your today and tomorrow
what is left to borrow?
one day more with these words
one day more with these dreams
one day more with this life
what is left of sorrow?
nothing
i have your hand
i have heart
i know your dreams
to depart in song
lifted in dance
i know your today
seek your tomorrow

same

silent on knowing
how yesterday to mend
actions hit harder than words
impacted a friend
i acted
how foolish i must have been
seeking a place to find
making amends
heart broken
hurting from hurting another
exploring a commitment
to a different life
i must attend the dreams of others
the fault of my actions
asking forgiveness
seeking the same
have and proclaim
my name in a different way
of one who seeks resolution?

here

simple treasures
found in life's pleasures
sunrises and sunsets
rainy days to grow
sunny days to know
everything will be all right
sandy beaches
spirits retreat there
words written with intention
saved for another day
slow dances
holding hands
candle light
in a life before
house full of shadows
no reason to go home
don't live there anymore
comfort here
to reappear in another life
before me
behind me

allow

i see you at a distance
in my dreams
in my words
your beauty captures
the breath i take to exist
the beat of my heart
remains in place
knowing ...
don't walk away
don't end today
what tomorrow allows
stay in place
as tomorrow deploys
as today existed
it is you i believe in
my dreams to provide
impact on my life
are everlasting
your beauty
your love
the reason
i smile

isn't

love isn't enough
to move your memory
holding on to history
my hand isn't worth taking
for another day
mumbled words
passing thoughts
my shadow grows smaller
in your dreams
while my muse
seeks asylum
undisputed
days go uncounted
walking away
beyond
what you could commit
better yet
nothing resolves
so quick
that I'm forgotten
a place in time
still and unafraid
silent in longer days
while words fade
depth and measure
of what cannot be

little

traveling so long
to find you
ages before i arrived
my dreams took hold
of this life
closer to heaven
in your presence
taking little
leaving less behind
moving forward
with you by my side
seeking the words
i can't explain
wondering
not in vain
loving you more
each day

control

ideas are peaceful
history not content
hearing the seasons coming
i celebrate what's left
love pursues my heart
my dreams need no introduction
they're alive and well
in a place between the shadows
hidden from the journey
my words fall silent
to your control
love insists on winning
a race already won
again and again
with nothing to mend
not losing again
gaining a friend
to love in the end
dreams fail to amend

daffodils

time has numbered my days
untold to me in this fairy tale
where i remain invisible
standing in a room full of people
crowded streets and musical beats
but no one to dance with me
sandy beaches and ocean glow
waking there to soothe my soul
common fields of daffodils
cut and washed for a table of one
life is brightened by their beauty
buttercups line them up
as spring arrives on time
souls swirl about me
interlocked into a world between
beyond what's in my memory
flowing words like a mountain river
still no one reads them
life is abbreviated into moments
folded into one another
no path i have chosen
no moment defines
who i am; who i become
vulnerable where i stand
my words fall softly on the limits of time
knowing these moments
this section in this life
could define a future
not in my thoughts
not in my dreams

not in my tomorrow
time cannot be borrowed
so long as the ground
is beneath my feet
i will press on

understand

what time allows
what dreams appear
what is forgiven
what disappears
silent talks upon the wind
a breeze beyond these years
around the corner
and disappear
into a new life
matters not
matters still
not easy always to understand
a journey made across this land
no terms forgiven
no time inherited
in time forgotten
about tomorrow
not just anyone holds my heart
not just anyone receives these words
my song is played
my dance swayed
from my troubled feet
i hear the beat of your heart
in my next step
i see you
in my thoughts
in my dreams
i live a good life

simple

the mist of the fog
translates itself
into a deafening barrier
i want to lead
through the darkness
through the complications of life
to sing songs unwritten
but the path of life is short
and i hold your hand
ever so gently
to remind you who i am
i have dreams
i want a beautiful life
i want to be happy
i want to see your smile
a simple being
a simple life
standing beside you

clues

ghosts i knew
hidden from my view
by the shadow of tomorrow
loving you still
many dreams reveal
courage i find in you
holding my hand still stands
precious moments advance
where my spirit can dance
don't step away
with such little to say
my heart remains close to you
spirits reappear
your love held dear
it remains clear
while i am still unloved
where i stand
alone still hoping
tomorrow reveals
a path for me to follow
don't push away
needing you to stay
folded into me
there are a few clues
i cannot refuse
your meaning to me

aligns

too many shadows in this life
forever my friend; i stand at a wall
i don't see the end
flowers that never grew
blossoms fail to mend
scared of what could lend
even though i feel your touch
you're so far away to send
a thought my way
while i have you here
sometimes you are not with me
a distance too far to see
on an edge
overlooking
what tomorrow can bring
what today allows
sets a path in song
what words embrace
my final debate
between these dreams
i have no choice
in terms of fate
call me late as time aligns

not easy

years fall away
finding a place
where a note was left
to explain a day
you stepped away
without explanation
a soft breeze
reminds me of days
when i heard your voice
of wisdom
of stability
in an unstable world
maybe the note is hidden
for days to come and go
maybe it's not for me to know
perhaps i never will
as days move on
thoughts have come and gone
it's never easy
doubt it ever will be
conversations but there is no sound
from your answers
no new thought
no new guidance
only from your memory
if there was only something to explain
about the journey you needed to take
putting things in place
but never to return
i just needed a few words
to bid you farewell

far

finding my place
in the tunnel of time
it doesn't matter
where you are
it's still too far
for me to reach
when the darkness has robbed you
can you see that i love you
can you feel that i love you
whispers fill the void of dreams
i wait for the touch of your hand
as the sun rises
in the picture of a new day
tomorrow seeks
what time allows
too often
you are too far from my view
too often
i cannot touch your hand
too often
i seek the shelter of your heart
too often
i seek the comfort of your strength
and, i am fulfilled by your courage
i want to lean into you
and you into me

music

dusk
honeysuckle permeates the air
clouds scrape the darkening sky
birds announce the end of another day;
half the moon hangs high
the spring breeze cools my skin
i gaze at the future from this hill
my music breaks
the sounds of nature
bruce springsteen spells out the streets of philadelphia
david gray waxes poetically about you being mine
the softness of spring lies in the air
though summer can be seen from where i sit
my skin hints of the brown tint
the kiss of the sun
my feet are free of socks and shoes
the lushness of the grass can be felt
as i traverse the landscape
to a chair of nowhere
except these words
a red ring forms around the natural satellite
the gray of night hastens the day
begs for the forgivencss
the day relents
from this ending
another begins
i wonder if you are thinking of me

another

spirits fold themselves into these words
stepping back from an eternal rest to show the way
paths untouched but driven clear by daydreams
the production of whispers
beyond the sound of music that created memories
i am yours and you are mine
finding ourselves in the infinite wisdom of time
what is or may be doesn't languish or exhaust itself
yet life flourishes taking newer ground
each day as we continue to discover one another
calling your name in my dreams
carrying your memory with me
as the day moves along
i remember in song
just how much i love you
time and forgotten of a place
left unspoken if words could go on
without some artisan meaning
they do; unequivocal to a standard yet set
prose and phrases
don't stand a chance in translation
my heart beats faster hearing your name
grows weary when i see you walk away
wanting to pull you close
exclaim in reverence in a crowd; how i feel
my spirit rises to meet the road
untold are stories left unfolded
yet will make perfect memories
in another day

untitled

mistaken not taken
my words find a place
vulnerable and weak
shy but not meek
upon the wind
letters fall
always i seek
among the many streets
where you might be
no photos taken
still have memories
of a lullaby
sleep well
as the wind blows into your soul
away from me
but i am there nonetheless
curious and unafraid
looking into your eyes
gazing upon your soul
eternity of my time
emphasis on my heart
light of my path
that sets my spirit at your feet
waiting for me to meet
tomorrow there is no defeat
in the song of a thousand years
already written
created and intended
for this purpose
apparent of this ageless love

woven into this blanket of life
warmed in this winter
cooled in this summer
the touch of your hand releases me
and i am free in this time

revelation

i can't listen to the whispers
yesterday has come and gone
tomorrow insists in yours
only hold me in your arms
there are no shadows
between us
yet i feel alone
waiting for you to join us
when well enough is on its own
no words will ever capture
dreams will never rest
if we walk in different circles
standing back watching you laugh
time has its favorite moments
snapshots from what was
dreams of what could be
tangled words
left hanging in the wind
i turn to go where you have been
where i cannot be
the noise of life
is overwhelming
but it's a brand new day
your kiss has revived my soul

light

i am slow in the darkness of your silence
i am distant in the loss of your touch
eyes are closed while the world is sleeping
knowing tomorrow i need you just as much
in the art of what's created
drawing, painted and song
i find your beauty among my vision
what is right
what is wrong
what tomorrow brings
i want to offer
what tomorrow brings
i want to dream
hold your hand while others are looking
pull you into me like it should be
i see the path laid before me
crowded streets prevent closer attention
the imprint on my heart
cannot be challenged or explained
i cannot refrain from your memory
you from mine or in between
no matter how dark the sky becomes;
you remain the light in my heart

i see you

i sit at this edge
finding a place for these words
shh ... don't look
allow the sun to shine for you
allow the moon to make it right
the stars reflect your light
the earth spins from left to right
seeking your energy
the wind blows from your direction
seeking a way from you to me
words find their way in song
knowing they will sing of your beauty
what is written to be said
whispers of what's ahead
paths go untread
if a future has no use
allow me to caress your spirit
allow me to stand by your soul
allow me to take hold of tomorrow
where shadows fall
what days intend
to make a beginning
never an end
i sit at this edge
looking at what can be
how time has interrupted
a space between
patiently i seek
what is not too late
as the days become days
dreams align with our fate

collide

sorting the stars
among the fallen stones
on paths unknown
walking toward my destiny
moonlight brightens the path
unfolds in the expectations of time
what can be forgiven - is forgotten
not worth the trouble
worried about what appears
as it arrives - interrupting
the space between two sunsets
what i don't know
i learn and make my way
through the streets brightened by people
i've yet to meet
trust that i know where to point this boat
on the deep and wide ocean
no path there except the light of stars
dark and long - the night is deep
as space retreats
to the inner corners of infinity
traveling here forever
from a forgotten dream
whispers not taken from the wind to begin again
collide in time
stones unturned at a winter's end
tomorrow comes quickly
mending a broken heart
muddled thoughts
of a blissful song
with no one to dance

allow

waiting to catch my breathe
remain the same
about a love story
about today
shadows cast
where my soul remains
yesterday gives way to today
loving you still
my spirit at will
hearing the words set pace
what tomorrow allows
i shall take a vow
to love you forever

talks

this is where our lives cross
this moment in time
my breath is yours
yours is mine
there is a story to be told
until we're old
quiet words and long walks
holding hands
generous talks
time unspoken
between us
time unfettered
between us
time mistaken
for us
held in place
dreams unfolding
as shadows go
quiet and forming
warm and appraising
what the day brings
what thoughts think
what whispers form
on these lips
in the morning

pace

no words absconded the truth
that evolves the life
whispered in the face of tomorrow
hope cannot be dismantled
in the presence of your positive spirit
love of life celebrates your smile
and there is no path you cannot take
but for the grace of God go with you
into this wicked world
place yourself with greatness
your soul is sweet
competition begs your position in this place
be solitary you do not dare compete
but with your team beside you
you peak out into the world ahead
along the path that lies at your feet
there are places to go
people to meet
so i bid you a fond farewell
into a world that is more gracious
in the light
of your precious soul

dew

writing these words
thinking of your smile
night is cool
pressing on
silent in my existence
silent in my dreams
in the morning
i see the light
flowers open to a mist of dew
spring brings
new life
except to this soul
except to this spirit
what i have are memories
with you
i have lived my dreams

longer

the other side as these words fall into place
i get shuffled to the back
to look at you from a distance
i can't find my way home
the stars are hidden from my view
while everything leads back to you
you have moved past these words
remaining distant
i see your smile as you look back to me
but your look tells all
hold still, reminding me of my sliver of time
my place, my pace slows
you get further away
i can no longer reach out to touch your hand
my words fall silent in the wind
that pushes me
holds my day still
i wonder how far we will get
before our horizons will no longer meet

stars

open your eyes in my dreams
see me across the room
the stars light the sky
your smile my heart
the journey we take
is not a marathon
but a stroll on a path
we do not know
the horizon meets our feet
you're the melody
in my heart
dancing to the beat
music plays from yesterday
the night pushes away the stars
the sun rises to meet the day
i don't remember
when i fell in love with you
i do remember
when i first kissed you

sunrise

window pane
settled dust
beauty in silence
beauty in trust
warm embrace
a subtle touch
trembling
if the future
holds true
expectations
don't disappoint
dreams make me smile
no hideaway
except in my heart
except in my soul
tired of the sunsets
ready for the sunrise
oceans glow
waves rise to meet the shore
a path at my feet
a good book
words for another day
to return

dawn

finding strength in my flaws
in my emotions
seeking what others seek
dawn of the day
in winter
in spring
without the words
i love you
without
gentleness of a touch
no more
no less
of this life is expected
to be happy
finding a place
where whispers are heard
clearly
not echoed
where my soul is cleansed
angel's wing fixed
to my spirited being
no bells to chime
no worlds to transgress
oceans deep
no spirits seek this world
the land of the living
returns me
to this place
looking at you
by my side

seize

beauty in silence
power of a kiss
beauty in truth
cannot resist
what's to become
what's to exist
in the parallels of life
in the parallels of love
separate but the same
together of the same soul
sharing the same heart
path to walk
souls depart
in the future
of coming years
i do not resist
the sun evolving across the sky
hope seizes the day
my words find their place
in your heart
and i am okay
knowing i am
dealing with today

sustainable

fear like no other
time doesn't retract
my mind is distracted
from the noise of this place
slow down to
a muddled motion
genuine fear
no control; no tears
step into a shadow
as the sun lags behind the day
silhouettes sink in succession
nothing to brag about
i should have left when i was 7
no path if you're young
vulnerable unattended
except by the bottle
or by the belt
expectations are not anything else
abandoned
tomorrow stands out
fear is not sustainable
not here; not in this place
i have grown to be what i am
i am not alone
i am not afraid
seeking these words
for my protection
not looking back
i step forward and away

begin

a new story
about tomorrow
about today
about what these words
fail to express
these dreams
fail to endeavor
i miss you
like there was never a sunrise
before you
i see you
in my thoughts
before you
i had no vision
i feel your touch
before you
i knew nothing of love
i feel the joy of life
where i didn't know joy
i cannot cry
when all i do is smile
i cannot walk away
i am supposed to be here
when i need someone
i think of you
what i intend to do
what i have done
is wander throughout life
knowing i would find you
today

intended

the darkness has robbed me
still tomorrow presses the day
sun rises and begins
awakes my soul from within
a thought of you
my first heartbeat
my first breath
clearing the still waters
for waves
as the silhouette of today
passes and gains strength
knowing sandy beaches
warm beneath my feet
cradle the burden
spirits from long ago
lashing out does no good
and my journey may end
before it began
smiling in sight of you
huddled masses of sincere intention
freedom of the world descends
all we're left with are our friends
what were stones
under the burden of life
are merely pebbles
in your presence

heart

when the wind blows
against my face
on a path i've yet to discover
a new life to understand
with or without each other
a piece of my soul
set to withstand
your smile in my heart
what tomorrow can bring
in the touch of your hand
what unfolds, what unwinds
what do we demand
in a life with one another
in a life from one another
music commands an ear
love demands a heart
tomorrow a today
left to start
a new beginning

memory

let me pick you up
i will take you out
wear my coat on the beach
early morning sunrise
wander into an unknown place
sitting on stools at a counter
looking at the promise of tomorrow
drinking a cup of coffee
autumn wind
holding hands as we please
strolling down the sandy sidewalks
softened by the breeze
muffled sounds of the ocean
please my heart
dare not tease
what today can bring
in terms of a smile
hand to hold you steady
as you remove your shoes
sand beneath your feet
pressure lifted from your shoulders
creating these memories
all this brings meaning to the world
i find no defeat in loving you
i smile knowing you're smiling
as my memory
doesn't retreat
my heart's upbeat
listening to the ocean
from a shell

defense

in defense of the stars
what heaven could be
lost in moments
to turn a key
endorsed
unspoken
but not asleep
in the quiet majesty
of the early evening

silence

words are powerful;
but not as much as silence

life is temporary ... love is eternal

starting a conversation: poems and prose
by
william d. sroufe

CPSIA information can be obtained
at www.ICGtesting.com
Printed in the USA
FSOW02n0923170817
37625FS